Thomas Pownall

The Right, Interest, and Duty, of Government

As Concerned in the Affairs of the East Indies

Thomas Pownall

The Right, Interest, and Duty, of Government
As Concerned in the Affairs of the East Indies

ISBN/EAN: 9783337186005

Printed in Europe, USA, Canada, Australia, Japan

Cover: Foto ©Suzi / pixelio.de

More available books at **www.hansebooks.com**

THE

Right, Intereſt, and Duty,

OF

GOVERNMENT,

As concerned in

THE AFFAIRS

OF THE

EAST INDIES.

The Caſe as ſtated and argument upon it as firſt
written, by GOVERNOR POWNALL, M. P.
in 1773, now reviſed.

LONDON,
Printed for J. Almon, oppoſite Burlington-Houſe, Piccadilly,
M DCC LXXXI.

THE

FOLLOWING TREATISE

IS MOST RESPECTFULLY DEDICATED

TO THE

SELECT COMMITTEE

OF THE

HOUSE OF COMMONS,
&c.

BY

AN OLD MEMBER OF THAT HOUSE

NOW NO LONGER A MEMBER.

PREFACE.

THE following argument, upon the cafe therein ftated, was firft written in the latter end of the year 1772, and circulated amongft feveral friends, men of bufinefs, under an idea that the Adminiftration of Government, meant to have taken up the affairs of the Eaft India company, by fome meafure to be acted upon: and it was publifhed in the beginning of the year 1773. In the courfe of the feffions of that year, Parliament paffed " An act for eftablifhing cer- " tain regulations for the better ma- " nagement of the affairs of the Eaft " India company, &c." Government, in confequence of the regulations provided, and powers given to it, fent a governor general and Council; and eftablifhed at Fort William a fupreme court

court of judicature : But the whole meafure was confidered as an experiment to be tried in the interim, until his Majefty's minifters could be at leifure, and fhould be able, to prepare fuch a fyftem for the eftablifhment of the ftate, of the company; and of the poor people faid to be conquered; as might be offered to Parliament for the final fettlement of thefe rights, and an eftablifhed fyftem of government, for that great and important objeft.

After the paffing of *that act of experiment*, I revifed the following paper, and made the feveral additions which are now annexed to it :—Yet feeing that the world at large was not difpofed, at that time, to enter into the queftion of right, or into the confideration of the meafures which muft be taken whenever it fhall be decided; I did not at that time publifh them, but put the papers in a drawer, where

they

they have lain to this time, and might
have lain to doom's-day;—Had I not
at this juncture (1780) been defired to
republifh what I publifhed in 1773,
as by not now being in Parliament, I
was fuppofed to have leifure to revife
it.

As to my leifure I have much lefs
now than I had, as I think I can dif-
pofe of my time much more profit-
ably as a man, than I ever did in parliament as a politician ; nor do I feel
myfelf difpofed to take up again matters of politicks, which are but matters of cabal amongft individuals ;
of faction amongft parties ; and abfolutely the mean while decided upon
and decreed, *through a peculiar opera-
tion of predeftination*, by minifters.

All therefore which I have done, is
fo far to accede to what has been defired as to fend thefe papers, as they
were

were written in 1773 to Mr. Almon,
which he may, if he thinks it worth
his while, insert and publish in a se-
cond edition.

THE

THE

RIGHT, INTEREST, &c.

THE exercife of the fovereignty of popul-
ous and extenfive dominions in the Eaft
Indies, have come into the hands of the Eaft
India company ; the revenues of thefe dominions are actually in the poffeffion of this company; and in confequence of power arifing
from this exercife of fovereignty, and of influence from this poffeffion of the revenues,
the fame company have as merchants, while
they acted as fovereigns, carried on an abfolute
monopoly of the commerce of one of the rich-
eft manufacturing countries in the world.

The profits of this trade have been fo great,
that difficulty and embarraffment have arifen
how to inveft, or how bring home the balance
of it.

The

The revenues were fo ample and abundant, hat Lord Clive, in the year 1765, writes in thefe words to the directors of this company in England, " Your revenues, by means of this " new acquifition, will, as near as I can judge, " not fall far fhort for the enfuing year of 250 " lacks ! Sicca rupees, (including your former " poffeffions of Burdwan, &c.) Hereafter they " will at leaft amount to 20 or 30 lacks more. " Your civil and military expences in time of " peace, can never exceed 60 lacks of rupees ; " the Nabob's allowances are already reduced " to 42 lacks, and the tribute to the king is fix- " ed at 26 ; fo that there will be remaining a " clear gain to the company of 122 lacks of " Sicca rupees, or 1,650,900l. fterling ; which " will defray all the expences of the inveft- " ments, furnifh the whole of the China trea- " fure, anfwer all the demands of your other " fettlements in India, and leave a confiderable " balance in your treafury befides. In time of " war when the country may be fubject to the " incurfions of bodies of cavalry, we fhall, " notwithftanding, be able to collect a fufficient " fum for our civil and military exigencies, and " likewife for our inveftments ; becaufe a " very rich part of the Bengal and Bahar do- " minions are fituated to the eaftward of the " Ganges, where we never can be invaded. " What I have given you, is a real not imagina- " ry ftate of your revenues ; and you may be " affured they will not fall fhort of my com- " putation."

If· the public enquires after the caufes, why
the company is under any difficulties notwithftanding this ftate, they are told of the
want of wifdom and 'power in the company at home; of mifchievous errors in the directors; of factions in general courts ; of un-
governable difobedience in their fervants abroad ;
of peculation of public treafure ; of frauds in
expenditures ; of falfhoods in accounts ; of
plundering, pillaging, and rapine, both public
and private ; of rapacious extortions in trade,
which have ruined the commerce and manufactures of the country; of tyranny, in every
exertion of that cruel fpirit, which has abfolutely deftroyed the country itfelf : all this to
the fhame and opprobium of the nation may
be true; yet thefe are but natural, I had almoft
faid necefary effects of a prime original evil
which they derive from. The firft origin of
the evil is, *that the merchant is become the fovereign*; that a trading company have in their
hands the exercife of a fovereignty, which that
company by its direction within the realm is not
adequate to, and with which its fervants (the
governors and others, as now conftituted without the realm) fhould not be trufted. The fuf-
fering a trading company of merchants, fo cir-
cumftanced and fo conftituted, to affume the
poffeffion of, and to exercife (however acquired
and poffeffed) fuch fovereignty in a manner un-
obferved, unregulated by, and independent of
the fupreme fovereignty of the ftate, is the firft
error. This is the original evil: and the man-

ner

ner in which it hath been exercifed is only a natural and certain mifchief derived from it.

But be the conduct of perfons interefted in the company and its affairs ftill fuch as it has been; be the conduct of men in power what it will; be the conduct of their opponents what it may, as to the Indian affairs; the feelings of mankind in general are at laft roufed to a ftate of alarm; they apprehend danger to the ftate. People now at laft begin to view thofe Indian affairs, not fimply as beneficial appendages connected to the Empire ; but from the participation of their revenues being wrought into the very compofition and frame of our finances; from the commerce of that country being indiffolubly interwoven with our whole fyftem of commerce ; from the intercommunion of funded property between the company and the ftate—people in general from thefe views begin to fee fuch an union of intereft, fuch a co-exiftence between the two, that they tremble with horror even at the imagination of the downfall of this Indian part of our fyftem; knowing that it muft neceffarily involve with its fall, the ruin of the whole edifice of the Britifh empire.

It feems to me that it is a matter of the utmoft confequence to the nation, that thefe matters fhould be coolly, deliberately, and difpaffionately dilcuffed. It appears to me, that in general courts of the company where interefted animofity is the fpirit, that in other great affemblies where

where thefe matters are treated only as the inftruments of party, they will never be fo difcuffed. I own, from what I have had occafion to obferve, I have conceived an opinion, that thofe perfons alone who are no ways attached by intereft to this bufinefs, who are by no means connected with any party that may hope to derive fome ufe from it, are the moft likely to examine it in that line of inquiry in which the public is concerned. It is not in the whirlwind of contention ; it is not in the thunder of debate, that truth is heard : it is in the ftill fmall voice, in quiet abftracted deliberation that it will be found.

At this crifis therefore, *in this interval between report and confideration*, I, an uninterefted, unconnected individual byftander, without any poffible views of intereft, with a fixed determination of taking no part in debate, with almoft a certain affurance of difapprobation from all fides, and from all parties on all fides, will ftate the cafe, as it arifes from and is founded upon the fame principles which I have had occafion to explain in cafes of the like nature.

I will endeavour to explain to the public, the relation and precife predicament in which thefe foreign poffeffions, and in which the exercife of fovereignty over them, ftands with the fupreme government of Great Britain. From this ftate of the cafe I will endeavour to point out what the government of Great Britain has
a right

a right to do, what he ought to do, and what it can do.

Previous to all confiderations of the poffeffions of this company, and of the exercife of that fovereignty which has come into its hands, the firft immediate attention is due to its exiftence as founded on its capital trading ftock. This confideration government hath wifely taken up, and hath done therein what was neceffary and what will be effectual to that end : The edifice is now fecured and founded on a bafe which will fupport it.

Whether now thus eftablifhed it fhall become, as a part of one organized whole, as a part of our fyftem of empire, an aid in power and revenue : or whether as an independant unannexed object of commerce, a drain upon our force and ftrength ; muft depend upon the regulations, upon the meafures, which government fhall take concerning it.

To enable the public to judge how far government hath a right to interpofe, how far it ought to interpofe; they fhould firft confider the predicament under which this trading company hath a right to go forth of the realm ; to export Britifh fubjects ; to trade and make fettlements *in partibus exteris*; to poffefs lands and territories ; and to govern its fettlements, factories, and fo forth.

When

When this matter is traced back to its firſt ſpring and movement, and thence again deduced through the various ſucceeding proceſſes of its operations and exiſtence; it will be found to ſtand upon the ſame grounds and baſe; to have moved in the ſame line as all other like emigrations and ſettlements *in partibus cæteris* have done.

There are the like powers of incorporation, with rights of the ſame nature; the like powers of acquiring, purchaſing, and poſſeſſing lands and hereditaments within the realm; and the like rights of property and joint ſtock; the like rights of direction and government; the like permiſſion of emigration and of tranſporting emigrants; the like powers of trading, making ſettlements, and of eſtabliſhing factories *in partibus exteris*, within defined bounds; the like authority to build forts and otherwiſe fortify their poſſeſsions; to make war and peace with the natives, not Chriſtians, where they ſhall ſettle; the like powers of eſtabliſhing government, and of appointing governors and all neceſſary officers, civil and military, as have been given to all other coloniſts and emigrants.

Whoever will compare the charters of the one and of the other, clauſe by clauſe, word by word, will find this unvarying ſimiliarity extend through the whole.

Whoever

Whoever attentively confiders thefe charters, will find thefe powers granted not only without reference had, but previous to grants made by government of territorial poffcfsions. In the charter to the Virginia Company, granted in 1611-12, is a claufe fubfequent to claufes granting all the like powers as here before mentioned, in the words following. " And finally we " do for us, our heirs and fucceffors, grant and " agree, to and with the faid Sir Thomas Gates, " Sir George Somers, Richard Harkluit, and " Edward Maria Wingfield, and all others of " the faid firft colony; that we, our heirs and " fucceffors, *upon petition in that behalf made,* " fhall, by letters patent under our great feal of " England, give and grant unto fuch perfons, " their heirs and affigns, as the council of that " colony, or the moft part of them, fhall for " that purpofe nominate and affign, all the lands, " tenements, and hereditaments which fhall be " within the precincts limited for that colony, " as is aforefaid, *to be holden of us,* our heirs " and fucceffors, as of our manor of Eaft " Greenwich in the county of Kent, in free and " common focage only, and not *in capite.*"

Thefe colonifts therefore, fpeaking of them in general, had a power of making and acquiring, and of lawfully holding and poffeffing colonies, plantations, fettlements, and factories, *in partibus cæteris,* within the bounds prefcribed to them for trading and fettling, without any reference had to territorial grants—and by virtue

tue of this lawful power they had an implied
claim of right to territorial grants of such lands
or territories as they may have acquired under
these powers, where such could be lawfully
granted.

The East India company, speaking of it in
particular, had this power of acquiring, holding,
and possessing " ports, islands, plantations, caf-
tles, forts, factories, and territories" within
bounds defined by their charter, and consequently
this implied claim of right to grants of such—
Which, their charter of 1661 says, shall be im-
mediately and from henceforth under the power
and command of the said governor and company, their successors and assigns.—Other
charters give them power to purchase, or lawfully acquire such.—The parliament in 1692
(see the journals) admits the company's claim
of property in their forts, towns and territories
in India.—At the union of the two companies,
the old company, before the surrender of its
charter, conveys to the new " all ports, islands,
" plantations, territories, castles, forts, fortifica-
" tions, manors, lordships, messuages, lands, te-
" nements, hereditaments, rent, and revenues."
This conveyance and transferring of property,
this lodging of it in the new company, is recog-
nized by the crown, who becomes a party to the
deed tripartite, by which this conveyance and set-
tlement is made: and that the united company
are *ipso facto*, and of right, capable of acquiring,
and holding forts, factories, plantations, &c. in

C the

the fame manner as the old compahy was, the tripartite covenant is a proof; for it makes and prefcribes regulations for all fuch as are, *or ſhall be poſſeſſed by them*, within the limits of their charter.

Now all thefe rights of poffeffion, and all thefe poffeffions, are held without any reference had to any territorial grants of the fame, other than the general powers of fettling and planting colonies within certain defined boundaries; which general powers of poffeffions are thus qualified, "the fovereign right, power, and do-" minion over all the faid forts, places, and "plantations to the king, his heirs, and fuccef-" fors being always referved," as is exprefsly ftated in the charter of the tenth of king William.

Thus ftands the cafe of all that fort of property, and of thofe poffeffions of the Eaft India company, which is fpecifically defcribed in the deed tripartite, whereby that company was framed, united, and conftituted.

This is the cafe of all fuch fettlements as may be made, under the like powers of emigration and fettlement, in countries where the native inhabitants have no fixed occupancy in, nor mix their labours with the lands; and where there is no eftablifhed known form of government, or communion uniting into a collective body, the feveral individual natives, and as fuch, having

ing a fixed and actual occupancy of poffeffion.'
This is the very ground and bafis, on which
ftands our right of poffeffion, in almoft all our
fettlements in America, and on the coafts of
Afiica.

This is the cafe of all thofe fettlements and
landed poffeffions, where a municipal inhabi-
tancy, from the acquiefcence of the powers of
the country, hath by degrees grown into a territorial poffeffion.

- This ftate of landed poffeffion and territorial
property acquired and held under the privileges and powers above defcribed; and made,
and fettled, *in partibus exteris* within the
bounds prefcribed, is the firft ftage or procefs of
the fettlement of colonies; and even if the
colonifts thus holding their poffeffions do not, *by
petition in that behalf made*, pray for teritorial
grants of the fame . or, if the crown does not
of its own mere motion, interpofe and make
fuch grants, and erect thefe colonies or fettlements into provinces; yet the property of the
poffeffion is good and valid in the colonifts
againft all claimants whatever, and againft the
crown with the refervation as above.

But in the hiftory of our colonies and plantations, precedents exift almoft univerfally—
either of the crown's interpofition of its own
mere motion and grace, by erecting thefe colonies or plantations into provinces, in which cafe

it

it always makes territorial grants of the lands ; or of the colonists first moving, and claiming such grants, *by petition in that behalf made* ; in which cafe the crown recites the petition, and makes it the ground and bafis of the grant.

The Rhode Island charter recites, that " the " original colonists did tranfplant themfelves " to the country of the Indians, and did there " fettle, add have increafed and profpered ; and " are feized and poffeffed, by purchafe, and con- " fent of the faid natives, to their full content, " of the lands, ifland, rivers, &c. &c. which they " fpecify ; and therefore they pray a grant of " the fame from the crown."—The crown, in the charter, recites this claim of right, and makes out territorial grants of the fame.

The fettlers in the colony of Connecticut, who had gone out with all the powers above particularly recited, applying for territorial grants, ftate their rights of poffeffion by faying, that the greateft part of the colony was purchafed and obtained, for great and valuable confidera- tions, and *fome other parts gained by conqueft*. They therefore pray for territorial grants of the fame, *by petition in that behalf made*. The crown recites the petition, and makes it the ground and bafis of the grant. Although, therefore, the Eaft India company do poffefs in full right, fo far as to bar all claims againft them, a property in all their forts, fettlements, facto- ries, plantations ; yet they may if they think fit,

fit, by petition in that behalf made, claim territorial grants of thefe poffeffions as of right.
And the crown is (as fhould appear from the
like cafe) bound *to make, all fuch further grants,
as may be lawfully made, and as fhall be reafonably advifed* ;—for fo I underftand the covenant
in the charter of King William engaging to make
further grants of all fuch matters *and things*, as
may be lawfully granted—fo, I fay, I underftand it, when in context with the tenor of all
the former grants to the company; and when
compared, by analogy, with all other grants of
the like nature to colonifts.

On the other hand, the crown, fhould it fee
caufe, " *and be reafonably advifed*," may, of its
own motion, interpofe, and erect thofe colonies,
fettlements, factories or plantations, into a province or provinces : yet fuch interpofition would
in no wife impeach or alter the company's right
of property, in the poffeffions above referred to.
The crown, in the conftitution and terms of fuch,
will, as of right, make territorial grants of that
landed property. The right and the property
would receive no alteration ; the tenure, inftead
of being of an imperfect vague holding, would
become thereby defined ; would be united to
the ftate, under the jurifdiction of the crown ;
would be holden of the crown.

As all acquifitions of territory and dominion
in partibus exteris without the realm, until they
are annexed to the crown, as dominions belonging

ing to the realm, may be difpofed of and alienated by the king; the erecting fuch acquifitions
or territory into provinces, annexing them to the
crown as provinces of the realm, would make
this material and effential change; namely, that
they could never more, by the king, be put under
any foreign jurifdiction; under any jurifdiction
whatfoever which the law and the conftitution
of the kingdom did not authorize. They could
never be alienated, ceded, or transferred to any
other ftate whatfoever, by the king alone; could
never be put out of the protection of the crown.

There is however a predicament of property,
founded on a very different cafe, and leading to
a very different conclufion. Where landed
property (even within the bounds prefcribed for
making fettlements under the privileges and
powers as before) is exprefsly within the jurifdiction of fome known and acknowledged ftate;
is holden of that ftate; is holden as feuds, or
in the form and by virtue of offices: there our
crown can in no wife interpofe in the property,
is not competent to make grants of it, nor even
to make regulations about it. It might as well
affume a right and power to make a grant of,
or regulations for the feigneury of the dukedom
of Aubigny, becaufe it is the property of an
Englifh fubject; as to interpofe in making
grants of zimindarrees, jaghires, and fuch like
holding of lands and territories, while the
fovereignty under which thefe are holden remains intire.

There

There is a third cafe of a very different de-
fcription, and which leads to a very different
confideration: it is this; where the acquifitions
of landed property, territories or dominions,
whether made by purchafe, treaty, or conqueft,
pafs under thefe circumftances, namely, that the
fovereignty of which they were held, is become
vacant, or is transferred—there fuch acquifitions, whether made by the fubject under powers
granted by the crown, or by the crown imme-
diately; both as to property aud dominion veft
in the crown—as being and reprefenting the
active principle of that organized body the
community.

In order rather to explain, than to prove this
propofition, I will recur back to firft principles,
and by a deduction from thence of the procefs
of this fyftem, fhew how the cafe arifes in fact
and right.

When any number of individuals affociate,
and form that communion which becomes the
fubject matter of government; not only the individuals in their perfons, but in their rights and
property, are melted down into the common
mafs of the commonwealth. This commonwealth becomes A ONE ORGANIZED BODY,
having a one principle of individuality.—The
property in the lands and other immoveables,
thus forming this common mafs is, *primâ
inftantiâ*, in its primary and original derivation
the property of the ftate; unalienable and infe-
parable

parable from that ftate in any part thereof, but by the will of the whole ftate : it is an effential vital part of the organized living body. This property therefore muft receive the mode of its exiftence, connexion, relation, and fubordination; its ufe and application as a part; from the nature and organization of the whole.

From this theorem, which is fimply the definition of the actual exifting ftate of political communion, derive, by neceffary concatenation of truth and right, the following propofitions.

Whatever individual obtains poffeffion, and becomes the particular proprietor of any part of fuch property already in the community, he muft hold that poffeffion, and be an individual proprietor in fuch mode, relation and fubordination, to fuch extents of ufe and application only, as is primarily confiftent with the vital union of the whole; and in the next place, conformable to the difpofitions thereof made by the whole.

No individual can by fale, gift, or in any other manner transfer his property to any one who by poffeffing it can be fuppofed to feparate or diffever it from the community of the commonwealth. •

Thus far of property, already part of the community of the commonwealth.

On

On the other hand, " Every man" (fays Mr.
Lock) " when he at firſt incorporates himſelf
" into any commonwealth, he, by his uniting
" himſelf thereunto, annexes alſo and ſubmits to
" the community, thoſe poſſeſſions which he
" has, *or ſhall acquire, that do not already be-*
" *long to any other government :* for it would
" be a direct contradiction for any one to enter
" into a ſociety with others, for the ſecuring
" and regulating of property, and yet to ſup-
" poſe his land, whoſe property is to be re-
" gulated by the laws of the ſociety, ſhould be
" exempt from the juriſdiction of the govern-
" ment to which he himſelf, the proprietor of
" the land, is a ſubject."

. Hence it is, that if any individual, or any
political perſon or body corporate, who is part
of a community, obtains leave from that community to emigrate, in order to ſettle *in partibus
exteris,* out of the limits of that community ;
yet acts, ſettles, and acquires property under the
powers and privileges, and protection granted by
that community ; and does, in his perſonal individuality, ſtill himſelf belong to that community ; all property acquired by that perſon
(which does not already belong to ſome other
government, or which by any juſtifiable means
is diſſevered from the government it did belong
to) all property, I ſay, ſo acquired by ſuch perſon, does *ipſo facto* become annexed to, as the
property of, that community to which the individual himſelf belongs.

D   This

This is truth and right in the abstract. Apply this right to fact in the constitution of our own government—and then the particular truth stands thus, that all acquisitions of territory made by the subjects of Great Britain *in partibus exteris*, whether by purchase, treaty, or conquest, if the lands of these territories are such as do not belong to any other government, or having belonged to any other government, are such that the sovereignty or dominion under which they were becomes vacant or is transferred, then both the possession of, and dominion over these lands vest in the crown, so as to be of the allegiance, and what must be holden of the crown. Let us view this truth, which we may now call matter of law—in the actual execution of it.—And first as to Africa: An act for vesting the fort of Senegal and its dependencies in the company of merchants trading to Africa (which passed in the year 1764) has these words.—" Whereas the fort of Senegal and its

" dependencies were by the late treaty of peace
" ceded to Great Britain, and are now subject
" thereto ; and whereas it would be of advan-
" tage to Great Britain, and to the trade to
" Africa, if the said fort and its dependencies
" were also vested in the said company, may
" it therefore please your Majesty that it may
" be enacted ; and be it enacted by his most
" excellent Majesty, by and with, &c. that from
" and after the passing of this act, the fort of
" Senegal and its dependencies shall be, and
" the same and every part thereof are hereby
" declared

" declared to be vefted in the company of
" merchants trading to Africa."

Now this fpecial act of inveftiture of thefe
lands and territories was deemed and enacted as
neceffary notwithftanding they lay within the
bounds, and are parcels of thofe territories and
dominions on which the company had a right
to fettle, and which by fpecial charter in 1672
had been granted to it, under the like general
terms, as the power of fettling and acquiring
lands in the Eaft Indies is given to the Eaft
India company.

See next the cafe of St. Helena, as deriving
from this fame maxim of law—in the words of
the charter of confirmation to the governor and
company of merchants trading to the Eaft Indies, of the ifland of St. Helena, granted in the
25th year of the reign of king Charles the
fecond.

" Whereas in purfuance of our royal charter,
" the governor and company did at their own
" coft and charge, erect feveral forts and for-
" tifications at Sancta Helena, being an ifland
" fituate in, or near Africa, beyond the line,
" and on this fide the cape Bona Speranza, and
" place a garrifon there, and were proceeding
" to plant and people the fame, and for that
" purpofe had tranfported divers of our fubjects,
" who were willing thereunto, to inhabit there;
" but our faid fubjects, inhabiting on the faid

" ifland,

" iſland, were lately in time of war between us
" and the ſtates of the United Provinces, by
" force of arms difpoſſeſſed thereof by the ſub-
" jects and forces of the ſaid ſtates, and the
" ſubjects of the ſaid ſtates had and kept the
" quiet poſſeſſion thereof for ſeveral months to-
" gether.—And whereas by the bleſſing of
" God on our royal ſhips and forces, under the
" command of Capt. Richard Maundane, the
" ſaid iſland, and all and ſingular the forts,
" fortifications, and other the appurtenances
" thereunto belonging were retaken from the
" ſaid ſtates and their ſubjects, and a garriſon
" of our ſubjects placed there, by virtue or rea-
" ſon whereof, the ſaid iſland and all and ſin-
" gular the forts, fortifications, erections and
" buildings thereof, with the appurtenances
" thereof *are veſted in us, our heirs and fuc-*
" *ceſſors,* in the right of our crown, and all the
" artillery, arms, armour, weapons, ordnance,
" munition, magazines, ſtores, chattles, and
" moveables whatſoever, which were there
" found at the time our ſaid forces retook the
" ſame as aforeſaid, do of right belong to us
" and no other.————And whereas the ſaid
" iſland hath been found by experience to be
" very convenient and commodious to our
" loving ſubjects the governor and company of
" merchants trading to the Eaſt Indies, for the
" refeſhment of their ſervants and people in
" their returns homeward, being then often
" weak and decayed in their health, by reaſon
" of thoſe long voyages under thoſe hot cli-
" mates ;

" mates ; whereupon our faid fubjects, the faid
" governor and company, have befought us to
" regrant and confirm the fame to them.——
" We therefore, of our fpecial grace, certain
" knowledge, and mere motion, have given,
" granted, and confirmed, and by thefe pre-
" fents for us, our heirs and fucceffors, do give,
" grant, and confirm to the faid governor and
" company, their fucceffors and affigns, all that
" the faid ifland of Sancta Helena, &c. &c.
" and them the faid governor and company,
" &c. we do by thefe prefents for us, our
" heirs and fucceffors, make, create, and con-
" ftitute the true and abfolute lords and proprie-
" tors of the faid ifland and premifes, &c. Saving
" and always referving to us, our heirs and fuc-
" ceffors, the faith and allegiance to us due and
" belonging, and our royal power and fovereignty
" of and over our fubjects and inhabitants there."

Under the like predicaments, without any material difference, ftood the cafe of Louifbourg; and
of thofe places in the Eaft Indies, which were retaken by the joint forces of the crown and company.
Louifbourg was given up and ceded at the peace
of Aix-la-Chapelle. Thefe Eaft Indian territories lye in the hands of the Eaft India company.

See next the cafe of a ceffion of property with
a transfer of fovereignty in the inftance of the
ifland of Bombay : the cafe is ftated in the charter, relating to the ifland of Bombay, granted
in the 20th year of the reign of Charles the IId.

" Whereas

" Whereas by the late treaty, between our
" good brother the king of Portugal, concluded
" at Weftminfter, the 23d of June, 1661.—
" the faid king of Portugal did, by the eleventh
" article thereof, by and with the advice and
" confent of his counfel, freely, fully, abfolutely,
" and intirely, give, grant, transfer, and con-
" firm unto us, our heirs, and fucceffors, for
" ever, the port and ifland of Bombay, in the
" Eaft Indies; together with all the rights,
" profits, territories, and appurtenances thereof
" whatfoever, and as well the property, as the
" direct, full and abfolute dominion and fo-
" vereignty of the fame, &c. &c. which faid
" port and ifland of Bombay, and the territo-
" ries thereof, lying and being within the
" limits of our charter, granted to the governor,
" and company of merchants, trading to the
" Eaft Indies: Now know ye, &c. We there-
" fore, by the advice of our privy council, in all
" the grants, matters and things herein con-
" tained, of our fpecial grace, certain know-
" ledge, and mere motion, have given, granted,
" transferred, and confirmed, and by thefe pre-
" fents for us, our heirs and fucceffors, do give,
" grant, transfer, and confirm, &c." The reft
runs in the terms and words as above.

Any ceffion of any dominions or territories
in the Eaft Indies, whereby the fovereignty is
transferred muft in like manner veft in the crown,
and fhould be (and I own, I think of right
ought to be) granted to the company, if fuch
territories

territories lie within the bounds and limits of their charter; according to the terms under which they already are empowered, to have and hold landed property in territories and dominions, holden of the crown, and of the allegiance of the crown with the reſervations as before.

The caſe of territorial poſſeſſions acquired by conqueſt, whereby the former ſovereignty hath been *aboliſhed*, is ſtill ſtronger—becauſe no ſubject, either individual, or body corporate, going forth of the realm to ſettle and acquire lands, *in partibus exteris*, under powers granted by the crown, with reſervation of ſupreme juriſdiction, dominion, and ſovereignty, can poſſibly erect any ſovereignty: or if any ſuch ſovereignty ſhould ariſe, from a temporary neceſſity of exerciſing ſome government, can ſuch ſovereignty act, or even exiſt, but as the ſovereignty of, or derived from the crown?

It is therefore both in fact and right, from the nature of political community in general; from the nature and ſpirit of our conſtitution in particular; true in law—that ſuch poſſeſſions in land or territories ſo acquired, and the dominions over ſuch, muſt and do veſt in the crown not ſo veſt in the crown, that the king becomes grand Seigneur and ſole proprietor, to grant the ſame or not; to grant the ſame in ſuch form, and on ſuch tenure, as he ſhall will and pleaſe. But ſo far only, that while the political property (if I may ſo expreſs myſelf) remains in the

the ſtate ; and therefore by our government in the crown ; the perſonal property remains inviolate in the ſubjеct acquiring it, if acquired under ſuch powers as before-mentioned. The perſonal property however, at the ſame time and for the ſame reaſons, muſt in the mode of having and holding, in the diſpoſitions and regulations of the form in which it ſhould lie, in the conditions of its obligation and ſubordination to the whole, muſt derive from the nature of the political property veſted in the crown, and muſt therefore derive from the crown.

In acquiſitions thus made, under circumſtances not ſpecially provided for before—ſome act of the crown, repreſenting the ſtate, as was done in the caſes of Bombay and St. Helena ; or of the ſtate itſelf, as in the caſe of Senegal ; becomes (of right) neceſſary in order to fix the property in the company ; the dominion and ſovereignty in the crown : and in order to form the true and conſtitutional connexion between the two, under ſuch modes of the one, and ſuch bounds of the other, as the conſtitution of the company, deriving from and depending upon the conſtitution of the ſtate, requires.

Let any one, by application of the reaſoning above, to the three ſeveral caſes before ſtated, conſider the three ſeveral ſorts of property which the Eaſt India company has acquired and poſſeſſes, and there can no difficulty ariſe in deciding, what government hath a right to do in each

each cafe, and what it ought, to do upon the whole.

Thus far as to property. What government ought to do refpecting dominion and fovereignty, requires further difcuffion and confideration.

When we learn, that nabob after nabob has been driven from the feat of government; that the new creatures of the Eaft India company are feated on the mufnud or throne, by the fervants and deputies of the company; that the fovereigns of the country are content to receive their government from the hands of the company; that they govern under the protection, command, and by direction, of the company; by officers and minifters named by, and holding their offices at the will and pleafure of the company; that the company is in full receipt and poffeffion, and hath the fole diftribution of the revenues of the country; that they pay the officers and minifters, the nabobs, nay, even the Mogul himfelf, what the company eftimates, rates, and judges to be proper; that the company is abfolute landlord, and proprietor of the lands for ever; that it directs what military forces fhall be deemed proper, and allots what part of that fhall be put under the orders of the nabob or mogul---and what fhall remain under its own immediate command: when we learn all this, and find it to be the actual ftate of the government of the country, who will doubt, whether the native fovereignty of the country be or be 'not abolifhed ? Notwithftanding therefore the

farce

farce of treaties, with the fiction of a nabob, the fact is, that the government of the country is diſſolved, the ſovereignty annihilated.

The affecting to be only the protector of the government of the country as an ally ; to be only the ſteward, not the landlord of the dominions of the ſtate ; the executing the government of the country, under its own laws, ſo far as deſpotiſm admits law, and by the miniſtration of its own offices and officers, was one of thoſe genuine ſtrokes of politicks, which true and original genuis alone always doth at once adopt and execute*. Nothing could be wiſer, reſpecting the internal ſtate of the country ; nothing more prudent, at the time, reſpecting foreign ſtates ; and nothing better underſtood, for the then preſent occaſion, reſpecting the relation between the company, and the ſupreme government of Great Britain. The hand of explanation, on the face of the clock, points to this oſtenſible ſyſtem---but when we look into the internal ſprings and movements, when we read the minutes, and the ſecret and confidential correſpondence‡, or advert to the undiſguiſed explanation of the ſyſtem, we find the company ſtating themſelves as ſovereigns, having dominions and ſubjects† ; ſtating what ſort of army is neceſſary " *to preſerve them ſove-* " *reigns.*"

* Thoſe who wiſh to ſee this oſtenſible meaſure explained in the true ſpirit of it, may read Lord Clive's letter, Sept. 21, 1765.

‡ See Report of Select Committee.

† See Lord Clive's letter to Mr. Rous, April 17, 1765.

We

We find then that powers and interests have arisen in the course of the existence of this company, which were not in contemplation at the first forming of it; of which there was not an idea; for which therefore there is not, nor could not be in the charter any provision. On the contrary, we find the Attorney, and Solicitor General, Mr. Pratt, and Mr. York, in the year 1757, are " of opinion, that it is not warrant-
" ed by precedent, nor agreeable to found po-
" licy, nor to the tenor of the charters which
" have been laid before us, to make a general
" grant not only of past, but of future con-
" tingent conquests, made upon any power,
" European or Indian, *to a trading company.*"
And we further find, that in all grants of powers of government, the crown always reserves
" the sovereign right, power and dominion to
" itself, its heirs and successors."

These powers, therefore, of sovereignty, (howsoever they may have fallen into the hands of the company, or in whatever form they may lie there) cannot be duly exercised by that company, without some legal and constitutional interposition of the crown; and in the words of the same lawyers in the same opinion, I draw the other part of the conclusion, that, " all
" those dominions, such as have been lately ac-
" quired, or shall hereafter be acquired by con-
" quest, must all, both as to property as well
" as dominion, vest in the crown, by virtue of
" its own prerogative, and consequently the

E 2   " com-

" company can only derive a right to them
" through his Majefty's grant." I beg here to
repeat that I underftand this in the fenfe only as
above defcribed—in the diftinction between political and perfonal property.

Under this diftinction, I fay, not only from
the authority above, but from the authority of
reafon and demonftration, that it is not only neceffary refpecting the property, but what the
government ought to do of right refpecting the
due order of government---that it fhould make,
in the cafe above defcribed, territorial grants of
the dominions, where fuch *may be lawfully
granted*, and as fuch fhall be *reafonably advifed*,
according to the claim of right which the company hath on one hand, and according to law
and the conftitution on the other.

The government muft alfo either minifter
and execute thefe powers of fovereignty (thus
referved in the crown) by itfelf and its own
officers and fervants; or create and add to the
powers of the charter a new office authorifed to
execute the powers and adminifter the rights
which it may thus delegate.

I alfo who really think, from the experience
of all times, from the time of Tyre and Sidon
to the prefent, that the greateft evil arifes " *when
" traders become princes, and merchants fo-
"vereigns:*" and who, by deduction of experience
in like cafes, do not think that thefe powers
                                                    and

and rights (to be held and exercifed at the dif-
tance of the Indies) retained in the immediate
hands of the crown will add fuch power and
influence to the crown here as fome apprehend
and fear---do think it right, that the fovereignty
and dominion fhould remain in the crown, to
be executed by the crown, while the property
and all the rights, privileges and franchifes
fhould be confirmed and more fully eftablifhed
in the company.

But in whatever hands thefe powers are to
be vefted, or however executed and adminiftered,
let us try and examine of what fpirit they are,
that we may from thence decide what ought to
be the fpirit of fuch adminiftration.

Although the fovereignty of the native government of the country within the bounds of
the dominion of the Eaft India company is
abolifhed and annihilated, yet the forms and
orders, the offices, and oftenfible officers of the
government remain---the tenure of the lands remains as it did; the rents and revenues as they
did;---the ftate of rights perfonal and political,
the rule of government, fuch as they were; the
fovereign power and direction however, the abfolute military command, the abfolute perpetuity
of right in the revenues, the protection of that
creature of the company, the oftenfible fovereign,
is held under a very jealous and exclufive power
in the hands of the company:---Although it
fuffers the government to be exercifed by the
nominal

nominal officers of the ftate --- yet it is: the holder. of the ftate in its own hands.---This fituation of the Indian ftate, and this eftablifh-ment of the European STATE-HOLDER --- is the precife predicament of the cafe under con-fideration.

Thefe circumftances of the ftate, and this eftablifhment of the STATE-HOLDER, hath arifen from, and ftands founded on various cef-fions and negociations, at various revolutions; upon the whole tenor of the treaties of peace which have been concluded on circumftances brought on by force of arms.

The precife ftate and predicament therefore of that fovereignty which hath thus arifen, and muft *primâ inftantiâ*, veft in the crown, is that of becoming STATE-HOLDER to a province, of which the government is left in its old form and ftate, and is ftill exercifed upon its old rules of adminiftration, and by its old officers of ftate and police.

Whether therefore the government keeps this power in its own hands, or delegates it into. the hands of the Eaft India company, if it acts *as what it is*, (which is the only rule of all moral and political action) it muft act *as ftate-holder*---it muft retain the fole and executive power and command of the army; it muft pre-fide with a certain degree of controle over the eftablifhment and execution of the civil officers
of

of the ftate :---and, to this end, it muſt of right
hold and poſſeſs, as it doth the revenues of the
public: it muſt proteƈt the dominions from without, and ſupport the government in vigour and
efficiency within, leaving to it all its own forms,
rules, civil eſtabliſhments, movements, and
actions, free and intire. It becomes alſo, by its
preſiding and controling power, the duty of this
ftate-holder to proteƈt and maintain the people
in their perſons and in their rights.---It muſt,
as the primary cauſe for which it exiſts, alſo
proteƈt the Eaſt India company in all its property, its rights, privileges, and franchiſes.

If it were in the ſpirit of our government to
take a precedent from the experience of hiſtory,
I would wiſh to lay before them the conduƈt of
old Rome towards Macedonia and Illyricum.
I take it from the words of a decree of the ſe-
nate, made upon an occaſion ſuch as the preſent
caſe exhibits.——*Omnium primum liberos eſſe
placebat Macedonas atque Illyrios, ut omnibus
gentibus appareret, arma populi Romani, non
liberis ſervitutem, ſed contrà* SERVIENTIBUS
LIBERTATEM AFFERRE; *ut et in libertate
gentes quæ eſſent, tutam eam ſibi perpetuamque
ſub tutelâ populi Romani eſſe; & quæ ſub regibus viverent, & in præſens tempus* MITIORES
EOS, JUSTIORESQUE *reſpeƈtu populi Romani
habere ſe.* " It is reſolved, in the firſt place,
" That the Macedonians be and continue free.
" That it may be known to all nations, that the
" Roman arms do not impoſe ſlavery upon free
" people :

" people: but on the contrary afford and re-
" ftore liberty to thofe who have been reduced
" to flavery : that thofe nations who were and
" are in a ftate of freedom, may hold for the
" future that freedom, fecure and pepetuated
" under the patronage of the Roman people :
" and that thofe who have lived under monarchs
" may from the prefent moment find thofe their
" mafters, more juft and more moderate thro'
" the refpect with which they muft look up
" to the fpirit of Juftice and moderation in the
" Roman people." And accordingly when
Paulus Æmilius, in confequence of this decree,
eftablifhed the Roman provinces in Greece—
*Omnium primum liberos effe jubet Macedonas, ha-
bentes urbes eafdem agrofque, utentes legibus fuis,
annuos creantes magiftratus ; tributum, dimidium
ejus quod pependiffent regibus pendere populo
Romano.* " In the firft place, by the power and
" authority of his command, he declared the
" Macedonians tobe and confirmed them a free
" people, having and holding, in the fame
" manner as they were accuftomed, their civic
" rights and landed property ; ufing and enjoy-
" ing the fame laws, under the adminiftration
" of magiftrates created annually by themfelves:
" and as to tax or tribute, paying but a half-
" fubfidy to the Roman people, where they
" ufed to pay a whole one to their kings."

Under fuch a fpirit of dominion the fubject
ftate would remain, not by its will alone *obe-
dient*, but by its gratitude affectionately *attached*

to

to the fovereign ftate. It would remain in peace, becaufe the fovereign ftate could have no motive for difturbing, but every intereft in maintaining that peace. _ It would remain quiet and clear of all cabals, becaufe no individual perfon nor no party could find its intereft, but on the contrary, would rifque every danger in forming fuch cabals; which cabals it would be the intereft of the fupreme ftate to crufh in their firft movements. A people in this fituation would remain in a fettled eftablifhment, becaufe they could have no motive for a change. The fovereign power of the fupreme government would be fixed and permanent: the fubject ftate would be eftablifhed in peace and the full enjoyment of its rights and capacities. Under fuch circumftances of the community—whereby the individuals found themfelves protected in their perfons and infured in their property— where the community in general was under a certainty of freedom in the direction of its induftry—in perfect liberty as to the difpofal of its produce—fure of enjoying the profits of that produce—the genuine fpirit of a landworking, manufacturing, trading people, operating in a fine climate on a rich country, would come forward in every effect of productive induftry; and would become, to a commercial ftate that had the government and protection of it, an inexhauftible mine of true profit, deriving in an increafing influx of ufeful, not an overflowing deluge of deftructive riches. The gradual accretion of money thus deriving, nurtures, and

F   extends

extends the induſtry; and forms and raiſes the powers of a nation: the latter plethorick influx *becomes a diſeaſe*, which, deranging the ſcale of proportion in all value, creates obſtructions and conglomerated inequalities; breaks out in luxury among the great; in ſpeculating tricking attempts *in making haſte to be rich* amongſt the middling traders, and in idleneſs and a total diſſolution of all *principled* ſubordination in the body of the people. This falſe ſtate of inflated health in the nation raiſes in the mind of government an inſolent phantom of power, which is known to its neighbours to be weakneſs abroad, but which ends by corruption in tyranny at home.

Over and above that, it is thus our intereſt to form theſe external acquiſitions into ſuch eſtabliſhments; juſtice calls for ſome ſuch meaſure as this to be executed. Some ſuch meaſure as this is the only atonement that the nation can make for the crimes which have been ſuffered, hitherto with impunity, to be committed by a part of it.

Since I wrote the foregoing, the government of this country hath adop'ed a meaſure perfectly ſuited to, and what might be ſo modelled as to become a baſis of, the very meaſure recommended in this paper—It hath by act of parliament appointed and eſtabliſhed a governor general, and four counſellors, in whom it hath veſted all the power civil and military of the preſidency of Fort William in Bengal; alſo the ordering, management, and government of all

the

the territorial acquifitions and revenues in the kingdoms of Bengal, Bahir and Oriffa; with a fuperintending and controling power over the prefidencies of Madras, Bombay, and Bencoolen : With a fupreme power of making war or peace; and alfo of making and iffuing rules, ordinances, and regulations for the good order and civil government of the fettlement at Fort William in Bengal, and other factories and places fubordinate, or to be fubordinate thereto, and to fett, impofe, and levy reafonable fines and forfeitures for the breach or non-obfervance of fuch rules, ordinances, and regulations. In the fame manner the king is impowered to eftablifh a fupreme court of judicature for the town of Calcutta, and *the factory* at Fort William, and the limits thereof and *factories* fubordinate thereto.

I fpeak not here of this meafure as it refpects, and may refpect, thofe places reduced to and become, in their eftablifhment and polity, Britifh communities—My reafoning only confiders it as it refpects the government of a predominant over a fubordinate country, fuppofed however at the fame time to retain its own internal conftitutional polity. Viewing it in that light, I fay, fo far as this meafure affumes a fupreme, fuperintending, and controling power, fuperinduced, *ab extra*, over, but not mixing with, or deranging the internal powers of, the laws of the country, or profaning (in the fenfe in which the people of that country conceive to be prophaning)

the

the national cuftoms civil or religious ; fo far as it holds and duly collects *the public revenue*, by rules, though ftrict, yet fixed and known, and fuited to the nature of the fources of that revenue, inftead of collecting the fruit in a manner that has well nigh deftroyed the tree. So far as it holds, wields and directs, in thefe fubordinate countries, *the power of the fword* to the purpofes of external protection and internal peace, to maintenance of the ftate of which it is the ftate-holder; fo far is it neceffary, wife and beneficent. So far as the fupreme judicature fhall act as a *court remedial, by the general principles of common juftice, accommodated in their application to the cuftoms under which the character of the people is formed, to the laws which form their civil morality, is conducted,* and maintains this juftice afcendant under the protection of the Britifh government: Thus far it may be made one of the greateft bleffings which a reigning government, having political freedom within itfelf, can communicate to a people under its dominion: but if the adminiftration of juftice, and the executive power following it, doth or *ever fhall derange the grounds of the old national cuftoms, or the fpirit of their civil moral ty, or the orders and cafts by which the people as a nation are divided and arranged, doth or ever fhall interfere with, and crofs upon the fundamental laws of the nation*, it will tear up all law by the roots, and under the cruel delufion of juftice, plant the moft wicked of all defpotifm in the extreme.

If

If that *supreme treasury*, which must neces-
sarily become the ultimate repository, as the re-
servoir of all the revenue, should, instead of suf-
fering the fruit to grow by its natural process,
instead of collecting it as only the *surplus* which
the people can spare over and above what is ne-
cessary to the support of the labourer, to the
maintenance of the stock of the manufacturer,
and to the payment of the interest of money
employed to conduct the trade and commerce
of the whole, *should, under ignorance in this
true policy, attempt to profit in the exertion of
the vague, undescribing, inapplicable terms of
the British municipal law, go to severe and extreme execution of Exchequer or Admiralty
proceedings*, there is not a miserable wretch,
whether rich or poor, who will not from that
moment loose *all right and security both in his
property and person*, all comfort, rest, and even
hope in his existence,

If the governor general, council, or judges
under any the like *wilful* or ignorant perver-
sions, should ever extend the controling and
superintending power of the predominant state
vested in them to persons and places, *which,
though subordinate to their factories, are yet
municipal in themselves*, by assuming to make
rules, ordinances, and regulations, which, while
they supercede the laws and customs of the
subordinate community, cannot apply but in direct Despotism ; *that supreme imperium which
the British nation means to hold in the ascen-
dant*

dant over the Indian government, will be the most transcendant curse of despotism. But if, on the contrary, according to the true intent and meaning of the Britifh legiflature; according to the fpirit of the Roman precedent; the law eftablifhing an afcendant government in Bengal, Bahar and Oriffa, fhall be fo explained and amended, That while this government holds the fword, it exercifes that power only by internal exertion in aid of the national government, or by protection againft external violence. If, while as a real protector and judge, it gives remedy and relieves by equity the unavoidable hardfhips which ftrict law occafions; if, while it exercifes this fuperceding, it leaves undifturbed and uninterrupted the national and cuftom and civil morality confequent thereupon: If, while it looks only to the collective revenue, it fuffers the induftry of the country to apply its labour in its own way, and fuffers the Bee (if I may fo exprefs myfelf) to collect and ftore and poffefs its own honey in its own combs, until the ftate calls for that part which the hive can fpare, and which doth and fhould go to the fupport of government. It will make the community productive in its labor, and happy in the enjoyment of the fruits of that labor. An ingenious, induftrious, thrifty people, thus made happy, will in return be conftantly producing, by a fuperlucration of profit in manufactures and commerce, a conftantly increafing revenue, the fource of abundant, permanent wealth and power to the ftate.

Nor

Nor is it of the laft confideration to confider, that where juftice and benevolence become the beft policy, as it evidently does in this cafe of our Indian dependencies, there is nothing in which the actions of a great nation can approach fo near to an all-gracious Providence, as in giving and difpenfing fuch powers of government to a nation under its protection, as to make that people happy, from whom in wealth and power it derives all the fruits of that happinefs.

That the Britifh nation may feel difpofed to do, and that the government of that nation may do what is at the fame time for its honour and intereft to do, that is, provide for the happinefs of a meritorious people, who deferve every thing from it, and who abfolutely depend upon it, is the fervent wifh and prayer of him, whofe zeal for the peace, liberty, and happinefs of man-kind at large, and not any party fpirit, any views of intereft or even vanity, hath led to write and publifh this argument.

F 'I   N   I   S.

www.ingramcontent.com/pod-product-compliance
Lightning Source LLC
Chambersburg PA
CBHW021437090426
42739CB00009B/1515